IN WHATEVER
LIGHT
LEFT TO US

JESSICA JACOBS

SIBLING RIVALRY PRESS
LITTLE ROCK, ARKANSAS
DISTURB / ENRAPTURE

In Whatever Light Left to Us
Copyright © 2016 by Jessica Jacobs

Cover art: *The Bracelet* by Carol Bennett
Author photograph: Lily Darragh
Cover design: Seth Pennington

Sibling Rivalry Press, LLC
PO Box 26147
Little Rock, AR 72221

info@siblingrivalrypress.com

www.siblingrivalrypress.com

ISBN: 978-1-943977-19-2

This title is housed permanently in the Rare Books and Special Collections Vault of the Library of Congress.

First Sibling Rivalry Press Edition, September 2016

IN WHATEVER
LIGHT
LEFT TO US

For my wife,
who trusts me
to write these things
as I saw them.

If Marriage Means Someone Who Will Always Come Looking: A Fable

Once there were two women, running through winter, through cold so constant there was only the myth of thaw. Their every step was a detonation in miniature, a brume of displaced ground cloud. And yet. Hair tempered to salt-spiked quivers, eyes lashed with tears flash-frozen, they were running alone along the river.

They ran neither from nor toward. But this is not the mystery.

One punched into a snowbank and brought forth a palmful unpocked by exhaust. Though thirsty, she offered it first to the other. Cold peppered their tongues, melted

into sustenance. *Who needs to walk on water,* they asked, *when we can run on it instead, can hold it for miles in our open palms and never suffer for more?* Yet in this cross-section of bantling January, this is not the mystery.

Stalled sky-top, the noon sun roused enough vapor to erase the day, to loose fields from their fieldness into confluence with roads, which were similarly undone. Each counted the other's strides to stay joined in time, kept pace with the other's breathing—*in*, two steps; *out*, two steps. But, on this bleared road, how to move together and still heed the boundaries of self—still have selves at all?

In the worst of it—minds heavy with the miles covered (with the miles still to come)—the mystery is this: They never once wondered why they were there, and never once wished to be anywhere else. True, even

in that expanse of temporary absence, in that swath provisionally stitched by the treed horizon. That place where, from a distance, they were two points awaiting the thread needed to bind a button to cloth, which would in turn bind the hem of field and sky.

So if she went missing, her love could follow and find her, each tied red ribbons to branches—a bloodless blood trail. If being bound as they were meant they could never fully lose themselves, then at least it also meant they could never be fully lost.

13<u>th</u> Birthday and Something Said to Wake Early

so I bellied out to the edge of our dock, fitted my fingers, palms
down, and rested my chin in their knuckled valley. Beneath
the black of the sky—a soft black, one in the process of giving itself

to morning—the water was hammered aluminum, dimpled and glossy.
But something swam against the current, surfacing at set intervals.
A gator? Two dark peaks, the terrible mouth submerged. The ruptured

lake resealing after it while far trees charred and crumpled
as the sun rose fast behind them, its kerf of light slashing toward me,
rutting the water as a buck does a tree trunk, leaving a fragrant, bright

wound. At its touch, carp leapt attacking minnows, each splash triggering
a band of explosions, ripples shattering against the dock.
And there I was, hovering

above a lake now boiling with fish. Herons made their long-necked dives. And me
in that body, newly a teenager, my legs and underarms freshly clear cut, razed
by razor blade, naked to the day. Breasts heavy and foreign as a knapsack. Desire

just as weighted—an insistent pull in my gut, flush in my chest. I wanted to be
anywhere else, I wanted to be, suddenly, with
others. The brine and swell of them, the splintered smell as I lay my cheek

to the boards, new stink from my armpits, which I had not yet learned
to mask, musk from the panties I'd dreamt in—a smell I could not yet
name, the warmth of it, the sweet sour ache of a body, opening.
                                                                                If fear

is metal in the mouth; desire, burnt sugar on the tongue; what was the taste of that
day? Of that fish-jumped, sun-stunned morning?
                                                        It was the green
of just mowed Sunday lawns, of mineral and lake muck, seaweed and algal blooms,

and, for the first time, an awareness of the taste of my own mouth, which I hoped
would one day soon taste another's. A passing plane was a silver mote
in the sky. *Take me with you, wherever you're going.*

There Ain't Nothing Like Breck for Stop n' Stare Hair

It's 10 p.m. Do you know where
your children are? Well, there I was

with the remote, my thumb a die punch,
a jackhammer's relentless up and down

through a world of possible
lives—*America's Most Wanted, Nick*

at Nite, To Catch a Predator—in search
of prey worth pausing for. I slowed,

though, not for shows but for
their interruptions: Bare shoulders. Wet

neck. Rope of hair glistening beneath a glistening
stream. Prell. Breck. So many ways to

get your hair glossy. So much skin
just off-screen

I tried to keep myself from wanting
to see. I rapped my wrist

with the remote; pinched the underside
of my thighs, behind

my knees—a girl's small-fingered self-
flagellation. I knew

only enough to know I should not want
this. So I called myself names, donned

shame as my hair shirt. Though I
never once turned it off. Or looked away.

Sex, Suddenly, Everywhere

∞

In shop class, that redhead with the jumpsuit zippered
from throat to crotch, trilling, *Boys,*

don't touch my zipper, until they trailed her like goslings, transfixed
by the shiny metal pull. The couple caught

naked in the science building bathroom. Backhand
whispers, *But I wouldn't even take my shoes off in there!* And how many

eighth-grade dance parties in the country club boathouse, some girl
in a corner crying about some boy, some boy nervously plucking

the wales of his corduroys, waves lapping—unheard but always lapping—
as I got freaked by the Pagan twins to a Boys II Men slow jam. Confused

girl meshed between two confused brothers, I tried not to stare
at the girls I wished against me instead.

∞

And every day those hallways: crowded cattle shoots, musked up
clusters of young bodies, slap of sandals, snap of bra straps, high sweet
stench of mall-bought perfume. My nose to the back of another girl's

neck, close enough to see a single strand, escaped, curling beneath
her collar, the gym class dampness between her shoulder blades. Sometimes
it was all I could do to keep my clothes on. To keep from moaning

aloud. Once a bucket—an occasional, embarrassing slosh over the top
if jostled—now a sieve, desire leaking from every pore. Which is why
I tried so hard to be harder. To use the world as my whetstone, sharpening

myself against each day. My body cried out for armor. Big boned,
broad shouldered, I was built for it: forced into a dress with shoulder pads,
I was the 80s' littlest linebacker. So I began to run, clanking

like a tank around cul-de-sacs. Began to climb, building biceps
strong enough to stiff-arm the world away. Even my heart grew
heavy, grew into one more thing to carry.

Sex Ed

Regardless, that summer they arrived—my gut-wrenched
need made visible, made just as repulsive as I'd imagined it to be:

windshields caked and rendered useless, radiators choked with the bodies
of black and red lovebugs, kissing bugs, fuck bugs, a horror movie

façade on every building, curtains of them unmoved by the breeze—
a mob, a building blackout. And I couldn't help

but envy them—those coupled bugs, coupling
for days, even while in flight—their lust

answered, each writhing insect partnered. Their desire was
singular, their purpose obvious; they didn't even have mouths to feed.

And That's How I Almost Died of Foolishness in Beautiful Florida

Nights, I ran golf courses whose water traps
shone red with the eyes of alligators and rang
with their falsely innocuous chorus
of chirps. The fairway grass was less
wilderness than carpet, whispering up
its pesticides. To get home, I memorized
street signs because every house
looked the same.
                              I have no doubt
that if I'd stayed—given in to the gravity
of expectations and inertia—I'd be
dead already, in my push to feel
something, anything:
                              neck snapped
over the bars of a mountain bike, or fallen
off one of the cliffs I'd fled to; too many
drugs, the wrong kind of women, or maybe even
a husband who'd never have known why sadness
was all he brought me.
                              Why I spent all day
staring at the lake, wading shoreline
where gators found their daily shade, thinking
it wouldn't be that bad, really,
couldn't be much worse than this
to offer myself to those jaws, those
daggered rows of teeth.
                              Its body weighting mine
to the muck-sunk bottom like a child
pulling in the cord of a favorite
balloon, saying, *Enough*
of all this air and sky. Come rest with me
here, deep as you can. Come rest
and dream of the life you might have led
if you'd left this place, this
falsely innocuous, this beautiful Florida.

What I Didn't Say During Those Years You Swore I'd Forgotten You

was that I was my own city,
my own New York, and you were a succession
of rolling blackouts, rolling through
me the way a shadow, each afternoon, unfurled
from the one ginkgo tree on my block: a rilled eclipse,
a dark slender bar—that mark
                              of division. On the corner where 11th splits
custody between East and West, we stood for six years,
a foot in either direction. The charge too much for any
wire to hold, we passed it from one to the next in a series of cascading
failures.
          Lights hushed from Houston to Battery Park.
                                Dark as any July 5th
of my Florida childhood: BBQs ashed, bins
clanking with empties, Roman candles gone
to soggy black paper. But once, alone on my dock, I
watched a meteor bisect the sky
like a thumbnail scoring the tender skin of a plum.
                                        You split me
again and again, your sudden shadow cast across the life
I thought I was living.
                    You swore
I'd forgotten you; I'd only wished I could.
So now, let me
          say this: Each time you returned, those nights
you tripped all the breakers, it's true: traffic lights failed and pedestrians
fled—tunnels clogged as bad arteries, bridges thrumming
above the glossy throat of the East River—but others,
                                        others stayed. Opened
windows and kicked off sheets, made love to the music of
battery-powered boomboxes on stoops below
where, off grills carried from fire escapes to sidewalks, neighbors
shared all the food they could not bear to waste. Such toothsome
smells from those feasts against spoilage, those burnt
                                offerings. And later,
                                    know there was
a moment when every office, every bar, every apartment

in my city emptied and all of us stood in the streets like the children
we'd taught ourselves not to be—hands on hips, elbows jutting
like wings, heads thrown back—remembering what had been
there all along: the night sky, suddenly visible.

Out of the Windfields

When the combines brought the fields
to their knees, it was like running through

an arid spreadsheet. Grid by grid,
dutifully, I logged my miles, the hours

on my feet, but kept true account of nothing
so much as my loneliness. Landlocked

Indiana. The place I'd come, god help me, to try
and find poetry. How long since I'd been held there,

even by water, given my weight to another
medium? All winter, the sky was desolate

white of a mussel's middle leeched by cold
of its gasoline glimmer. Static

landscape, untongued by tides. No dunes,
just windrowed cornstalks

crusted with snow. Yet constant
as lighthouses were the turbines. Idle,

they were sky-flung starfish
far from the sea, but moving they were

majestic, amphibious animals in their proper
element. Able to arc into the unseeable and return

with power. For three years, I tried to do the same.
But instead was desiccated, field-stripped, brittled

down to parts. All I could do was write until my sentence
ended. And in my final Midwestern week:

there you were. Beside me as my headlights slid
the storm-slick streets. Submerged

together without stars or streetlights, a turbine's
red light pulsed its beacon through the rain. Beneath it,

your hands bound me back together. In answering
prayer, I folded myself into the footwell; knelt

between your knees. And my mouth
to you was every water

I'd ever tasted: clean shock
of snowmelt in an alpine pond; tongue cased

in ocean's wetsuit of salt; green and mineral
of a springfed lake

—but most of all,
chlorine's high bite in the throatback

of every Florida pool in summer, the water
so bath-warm, so body-kindred, that entering

was like sliding into another skin—skin
that entered you back.

When Your Surgeon Brought Snapshots
to the Waiting Room

People say eyes are the windows
and all that, but turns out it's actually a pithy incision
into the navel, through which doctors spelunk
the world's smallest camera for the world's
weirdest home movie. After years of waiting, this
                    was our first full week together. Your body
was still a new thing to me. And here
                        was your right ovary,
ash gray and threatening rain, brindled by firebrick veins. Fat, a cluster
of discarded yolks. And your uterus, an unblossomed pink
peony, crawling with fibroids invasive
but benign as a swarm of white ants. This was not the garden
you'd abandoned in Kentucky for a patch
of dry Arkansas earth—certainly not
the garden you wanted *us* to grow.
                        Somewhere, off-screen,
the fist of your heart performed its steady squeeze and release, just
as my hands had in my lap since you were wheeled away, as they had
by my side while pacing between chairs bolted to the floor, had all along
the scuffed anonymous halls, up and down the entrance ramp
with its slide-and-hush electric glass doors.

When they finally let me back, I wanted to report
that inside you I'd seen a vision of a vast cathedral, or one of those
underground cities, complete with chapels, wineries,
and rec rooms. But, really, what I saw
                    was a small apartment in a bad neighborhood,
the one lent to us by a friend for that month
of your recovery. Its air tanged by new
paint. Its kitchen housing no more and no less
than two bowls, two plates, two forks, two spoons. Our
bedside tables, overturned bins; our first shared bed
an inflatable with a slow leak, where—despite your pain, despite
your nausea—we managed to find each other. Where
before sleep, we'd watch sitcoms on a cell phone
propped against my thighs: tiny figures living out tiny lives
on a screen smaller than a pack of cards, in homes

far better provisioned than ours; though watching them,
in their many rooms, (stale air whispering
from the mattress, our backs growing closer
to the floor); I couldn't see a single thing I wanted
more than this.

Post-Op, Still Out of It, You Said, *I Would*

you know, if we aren't assholes, I'd marry you.
We'd known each other, in that moment, six years
yet spent fewer than two weeks together. *You fill my heart with koi*
and dahlias, you said, which took me back
                              to the backyard pond
my dad mucked out each weekend, pumps clogged with
lake silt and clam shells, water brown as a drainage ditch.
                                        But the koi
persisted, bright as still-wrapped birthday gifts. The emissaries
of better places.

          Like later, when we visited that Big Sur inn, red dahlias
out front wide as the plates from which we ate barbecue to bursting. Each
floret a deeper red at its center
                          —How many states have we passed through?
How many miles have we driven?—
     Since we're not young, weeks have to do time
     for years of missing each other—
                              or like that painter's studio
in Taos with his triptych the yellow-gold of the dahlias
you'd envisioned, koi swimming the canvas; your dream made
manifest, sunset pouring past the mountains
to deepen the tones.
          Past midnight, we drove back down to Santa Fe.
Along the high desert road, the city lights ahead
were a grounded planetarium, abundant as the lightning
bugs we saw barber-poling every grass blade
in Tennessee.

          That having you
                    as my witness would make of this life a shared
palimpsest—the already lived
life still shining through, would make our past into a series
of parallel presents, I couldn't have known, but sensed somehow.

                         Which is why, even in those early days,
in the whiteness of that hospital bathroom, the one I'd nearly had to carry you
to, the one whose white tiles were so bright it was as though our eyes

were not open but closed and it was not the tiles we saw
but their after-image—a brightness of which you, with your wan face
and alabaster arms, were a part—when your pelvis tipped
    like an over-full bedpan
to ribbon your inner thigh with blood, I could do nothing but
                      comfort you and clean you as if
you were my own. Because you were, even then.

Curly, My Tangler

"Other lovers want to live with particular eyes; / I only want to be your stylist."
—*Pablo Neruda*

∞

The final day of the picking season, rocks breech
the grassy path and catch the wheels of our wooden barrow,
which knocks with a collecting box and two

flat-bottomed scoops, tipped with iron tines. In the last
of the unpicked patches, greenly adrift
in the blueberry barrens, we rake uphill: As you bend

tending to the lowbush fruit, your hair
hangs nearly to the branches. A rasping, faint
resistance in my palm, small pops as berries leave

their stems to mound the rake, weighting its passage.
The roll and fall of them into the crate. We rake gently,
with the tips, where the tines have the most give.

∞

Last night, from the small bathroom, you called
my name, asked me in.
>   *My mama's the only one who ever*
>   *brushed out my hair. But you're my wife.*
>   *You should know.*
I began at the bottom, your curls separating
with the thick sound of good cloth tearing.
>   *Do you see why I had no friends*
>   *when I was little? My mother would brush out*
>   *my hair each day before school.*
I eased my fingers, for the first time,
all the way through; asked how that felt for you.
>   *Vulnerable.*
Shimmering out beneath the overhead light—a climbing
of kudzu, a symphony of trumpet vines—your hair revealed itself.
>   *It was like velcro. Anything would stick in it—*
>   *bubble gum, spitwads, pencils. I'd come home crying*
>   *and mama would hold my ugly, frizzy head*
>   *and say, Baby, they're just jealous.*
>   *As though her love could make the lie so.*

∞

Our lips are blue, our teeth. Returning to the farmhouse,
we pass endless berries left on the branch.
Nature made for such abundance, for enough
to let the fields reseed themselves, for more

than we can possibly eat—when it comes to you,
your mother and I have this kind of love
in common. I hold your hand past the poplars and pines,
past the rough wood boxes of bees on the roof, my wife,

whose hair is the shade of farm fresh yolks, the color of
things rich on the tongue. Whose hair sings the plaintive
song of bed springs. Whose hair is smoke drifting
from a village of chimneys, corkscrews enough

for a thousand bottles of wine. A ski slope of s-curves,
a grove of twirling maple keys, every playground slide
worth sliding. Before a rapt audience,
a company of ballerinas cambers their hands

to trace out, in the air, your hair; my dear angora
goat, my cloud of bats spiraling from the cave.

Though We Made Love in the Afternoons

we fought each night in the smallness of our rented room, escaping
into New Mexico mornings shocked and squalled by two magpies
protecting a hidden nest. *Desert penguins*, we called them—
larger than jays but smaller than ravens—those words
                                        not quite right,
                              certainly not enough,
but to describe a thing not yet known,
comparison is sometimes the closest we can get:

              A year earlier,
hobbling through our first
ever weeks apart—you, in Tennessee; I, in Montana—lovesick
as teenagers—the only place with reception
was a field drowsed at dusk by bees. I stood for hours
amid their slow circling, still as I could, so your voice could find me.
                        There, in someone else's mountain homestead,
another nest. Tucked in a crook, it held four newly hatched
robins, their beaks white as the inside of orange rinds; bodies
like muscles stripped of skin, twists of gray-red flexing. Their heads—
awkward pincushions, mohawked—lolled
the twig walls, eyes sealed, mouths gaping. Below,
a girl with hair streaked pink (she emphasized the "and-a-half"
when she told me her age) swung in a hammock
looped from their tree to a shattered-glass greenhouse.
                                        Because she
already existed, she was more than the child we
imagined, but less, too, in that she was blemished by being
not ours.

              Just as the years we weren't yet together were both
better and worse than those ahead when one of us
will die while the other must stay and remember. Better
in that we did not yet know that magnitude of loss; worse,
in that we did not yet know what we would one day have
to lose. Yet, still, we bicker about nothing
and risk everything. Let us instead
be those fledglings, those new things. Be
that thin-ribbed nest of four-chambered need: Let us

guard and soothe and feed. Accept the other's
imperfections—and our own—as just the right type
of decay. Please, say you'll stay with me
until nothing is finished, until we weather
                              beyond measure of words.

∞

A Question to Ask Once the Honeymoon Is Over

Big around as my bike helmet and high as my ankle, the box turtle
was halfway from my side of the road to the other. The warm
sun felt delicious; my legs, strong. It was almost
to the center line. I hadn't been passed
by a car for miles. Figuring
if it was still there, I'd
pick it up on the way back, I cycled past.

                            Years before,
the woman across the street was shaped like that turtle,
or more like a toadstool, really, squat bell
of a body atop the thin stalks
of her legs, milky and bare beneath her
frayed black housedress. It hurt her to move—clear
even from my second-story window—so she brought
her trash out in increments, in small, bursting
grocery bags. She tossed each out the door onto the porch, then
nudged them, one step to the next, before easing—carefully,
painfully—herself down, a step at a time. Then she toed them,
finally, slowly, slowly into a crumpled heap at the curb. I left
my window to help; then took her trash out every week after.
                                 That story—
                    I hadn't yet
                            told it to my wife, had I?

                  But there was the turnaround
quicker than expected and I spun
to find a beat down bus trailed by all the fuming cars
that hadn't passed me.
                Steadying my handlebars against the wind,
I rode back hard, zigging around crushed squirrels and tire-splayed birds.

             The turtle
was just where I'd left it, but with
the top of its shell torn away. The dead turtle,
a raw red bowl, its blood slashing the twinned yellow lines
into an unequal sign,
          as in $a \neq b$, as in thinking about doing the right thing

is not the same as doing it. As in, how many times
did I watch that old woman shuffle bags down the stairs
(*really, how many?*) before I went from watching
to helping? As in, with my wife beside me
I am the woman who does not hesitate
to lay down her bike and give a small life
safe passage. As in, I biked slowly
home, told no one. As in:

>   Will she love me
>   less when she learns
>   I am not equal
>   to the person I am when she is watching?

In the First Fall of Our Marriage

Though I want to give you
only kindness, there's often an age between what I want
                                                  and who I am.
Yet how many times can you cry on my chest before something
good grows there?
                  Redwoods thrive in acid soil; summon
that weight, those stiff-fingered roots
to skewer my ribs and prime the rusted pump
in my chest. Into that age, let me
                                grow: a ring for each year, marking
boom and drought and flood. Let me anchor further, into
your roots; make me part of something
greater. Let me grow strong enough
that even when fallen
        I can be of use to you—
                                rough lumber for rafters and joists, a roof
for the drum of this evening's insistent rain. A cross-section
from my trunk set to spin on the phonograph—a record
of what has passed, playing the music of what
is to come. A song for each year
                                I'll learn to love you better.

In a Thicket of Body-Bent Grass

Arkansas is aspic with last-gasp summer, making running
like tunneling: the trail's air a gelatin
of trapped trajectories.

                         Yet deer float the twilight field,
ears periscoping the woody browse.
                              Trusting themselves
to thick cover, bucks bed alone
in deadfall and ditches. But females
gather where wind can breathe in
a predator's scent. Forelegs origamied in a mantis prayer,
they are poised to spring even when sleeping,
survival a balance between stillness and startle.

                                I stop, kneel, stalk
along blowdown of sumac and hackberry, cowlicks of crab grass.
Eye-level, the field is messy as a made bed unmade
by love, my hands greened and musked
from ungulate scat and piss. The deer—dark hillocks merged
with their shadows—welcome the animal
                               I've become, offer
an abandoned bed, matted and dusky as the sweated twists
at the base of your head those mornings you wake to thank
death for conceding another day. For the slatted light bugling
through the shades. For my palms to your breasts, my breath
to your neck.
           Here, though,
                 tonight, creature
in another creature's bed, I am taking
just a moment to be an animal alone
in my own head. All while you, I know, are home,
trying not to look for me, again,
out a window grown so dark it just reflects.

Forgive me. I'd grown so used to being lonely.

                        But, love, the sun has lived
barely half its life. There's time. It's taken half of mine to learn

the only way to make anything matter
is to have you there
                    to witness it. Wait.
            I'm running home. There's time.
                                        Tell me there is.

My Winded Love, My Sweet Shuffler

∞

When, on this looped trail,
you scuffle left (trying, always trying) and I run
right, it means running both
                                                away from
and back toward you. Disappearance and return:
A way to practice death; a daily way
to experience resurrection.

∞

Without a shirt, air eddies my ribcage. Without a watch,
no cultured clock time. Just poplars casting their long lines
of shadow, swallows ceding bats the sky. Without shoes,
the damp earth eases up to meet me, my steps quiet enough
the deer only quiver at my sudden scent—one, a fawn so young
its flanks are still licked dark by its mother's tongue.

                                                Earlier,
beneath our cool blue sheets, I brought my mouth to you
before your eyes had even opened;
                                        you said, *In my dream, you were
inside me. Did you know it? Were you there, too?*

∞

In these woods, winter is a brown room, and here we are, inside it
together. Above, the sky is stained glass cut by a leading
of brown branches. Between the trunks, a thousand blue doors.
We are in need of no keys. Behind one, the light is on
the river where gulls rise like ashes
from the sun's setting
fire.
    Do you see it,
                too?
                        My eyes strain
around each corner, ears hunt
for your returning step.

∞

No matter how many times
this running apart
to come back to each other
works, there's always a moment I'm sure
I've lost you. A moment my head goes
dark.
       But from behind the birches, there
you are, high-stepping
up a hill, panting a bit, yelling
my name, flushed, and happy.
                            We
are on the forest's far side. This day is well
on its way to the next.
                    Whether it's yours
or mine, we'll turn and return
as one—with a shared pace, a shared
                direction—continuing on
           together in whatever light
                        is left to us.

Because You Waited for Me to Fly Your First Kite

Let our love be this clutch
of dogs off-leash: the preen and posture, snort
and snuffle, of saying, *I smell you*
and, therefore, know you. The rolling
on the backs and baring of the bellies.
And the tails! An exaltation of metronomes,
                    keeping time for their joy.

If this summer is a body,
                    let me be its tongue.
Tasting the green tang of the spittlebug nests
foaming the oat grass, the iron of this
good dirt. A tongue to lick the salt
from your upper lip, the rosary of sweat
risen on your chest. A tongue to tap
the top teeth and suck back like a wave
whose tide rolls out through lips pursed
as though for a kiss.
                    Listen
          again: *Thank you.*

As in, thank you, please,
          let me be this kite
lifting from your hands—ruffled nylon paradise
bird, with its taut spine and cross spar, the pop
of its ripstop sails, snap of its translucent tails.

                              Give me
the grand view: white water and mountains; but mostly
of you—head thrown back, face to the sun, holding
my traceline: tethered to you,
always, responding to the slightest
tick of your fingertips. Let me be a kite that trusts itself
to the sky. Yes, gravity is inevitable

as death. But why let that desecrate
                    even a moment of this flight?

Notes

"And That's How I Almost Died of Foolishness in Beautiful Florida" takes its title from a line in Mary Oliver's "Alligator Poem."

In "Post Op, Still Out of It, You Said, *I Would*," the italicized section is a quote from the third section of Adrienne Rich's "Twenty-One Love Poems."

"Curly, My Tangler," is a phrase from Pablo Neruda's "Sonnet XIV," as is that poem's epigraph. The final section owes a debt to Charles Simic's glorious poem "Breasts."

Acknowledgments

I would like to thank the editors and staff of the following publications, in which these poems first appeared:

Brain Mill Press:
"Ain't Nothing Like Breck for Stop n' Stare Hair"

The Collagist:
"And That's How I Almost Died of Foolishness in Beautiful Florida"
"Out of the Windfields"

The Heartland Review:
"If Marriage Means Someone Who Will Always Come Looking: A Fable"

The Missouri Review:
"When Your Surgeon Brought Snapshots to the Waiting Room"
"Though We Made Love in the Afternoons"

THRUSH:
"13th Birthday and Something Said to Wake Early"

Washington Square Review:
"Post-Op, Still Out of It, You Said, *I Would*"

My thanks, too, to Bryan Borland and Seth Pennington, publishers, dear friends, and cheerleaders extraordinaire, as well as the astute SRP interns: Ellie Black, Emily Holmes, Carl Napolitano (yay, bugs!), and Allison Price. Gratitude to the artist Carol Bennett, who generously allowed *The Bracelet* to grace this book's cover. If these poems have improved from their early drafts, much of that is due to the generous feedback of Matthew Olzmann and Danielle DeTiberus. And, to Nickole Brown, these poems, even as they go out into the world, are and have always been for you.

About the Poet

Jessica Jacobs is the author of *Pelvis with Distance* (White Pine Press), winner of the New Mexico Book Award in Poetry, an Over the Rainbow selection by the American Library Association, and a finalist for the Lambda Literary Award and Julie Suk Award. An avid long-distance runner, Jessica has worked as a rock climbing instructor, bartender, editor, and professor, and now serves as faculty at Writing Workshops in Greece. She lives in Asheville, North Carolina, with her wife, the poet Nickole Brown. More of her poems, fiction, and essays can be found at:

www.jessicalgjacobs.com

About the Press

Sibling Rivalry Press is an independent press based in Little Rock, Arkansas. It is a sponsored project of Fractured Atlas, a nonprofit arts service organization. Contributions to support the operations of Sibling Rivalry Press are tax-deductible to the extent permitted by law, and your donations will directly assist in the publication of work that disturbs and enraptures. To contribute to the publication of more books like this one, please visit our website and click *donate*.

www.siblingrivalrypress.com

CPSIA information can be obtained at www.ICGtesting.com
Printed in the USA
BVOW08s2300280916

463077BV00007B/4/P